The Story of Amy Johnson...

Little Wings

F.J. Beerling

Illustrated by Gareth Bowler

Copyright © F.J.Beerling 2016
Published by Miss Potter Ltd

Published by Miss Potter Ltd © 2016

ISBN: 9780993384233

All rights reserved.

No part of this book shall be reproduced, stored in a retrieval system, or transmitted in any form by any means, electronic or mechanical, including photocopying, recording, or by any information retrieval system without prior written permission of the publisher.

F.J. Beerling and Gareth Bowler asserts the rights to be identified as the author and illustrator of this work in accordance with the Copyright, Designs & Patents Act, 1988.

For commissions and queries email
misspotterltd@gmail.com

Special thanks to

Michele Beadle, reader assistant at Hull History Centre, for verification of the historical content in this book.

Printed in the UK

Although every precation has been taken in the preparation of this book, the publisher, author and illustrator assume no responsibility for errors or omissions. Neither is any liability assumed for damages resulting from the use of this information contained herein.

Josie the Jet was afraid to fly, and she was scared of heights,
Not ideal for a passenger plane, built for holiday flights.

"It's just no good," cried Josie,
As into the hangar she backed.
All she needed was reassurance;
It was confidence that she lacked.

Then dear Old Bob the bi-plane, who was teaching Josie to fly.

Just flew in from Manston Airport and saw the little jet cry.

So Bob, had an idea that was sure to make her feel better.

First he had to stop Josie crying, the floor was getting wetter.

As Josie cried, the cleaner arrived and began to mop the floor.

Her tears had made a little puddle, that reached the hangar door.

"Don't you worry," cried Bob, "well soon have you up in the sky.

You just need to believe in yourself, then you'll be flying high!

Josie felt much better now,
 She even ventured outside.
"I WILL fly those holiday makers,"
 The little jet replied.

So she fired up her engines and taxied down the runway,
Almost hitting the Turbo Twins, as they were heading their way.

"Oh dear," cried Josie, panicking, as she turned herself around.
The Twins teased and laughed at her, as she skidded along the ground.

So she headed for the hangar, and hurried back inside.
Then backed herself into a corner: Josie wanted to hide.

"Don't you worry," cried Bob,
"Your propellers will get in a whirl!!
"But the Twins are right," sobbed little Josie,
"I am just a silly girl."

Old Bob smiled, then he cried: "I'm going to tell you a story,
About a lady, who against all odds, flew herself into glory!"

As Bob coaxed Josie back outside, and into the summer sun,
The cleaner had finished mopping the floor and was chewing on a bun!

And so Bob said to the little jet: "Amy Johnson was her name,
All she wanted to do was fly, but landed herself in fame."

"How did she do that?" quizzed Josie,

"By being a woman that's how!

Women travelled mostly as passengers; not pilots, like they do now."

Josie looked a bit puzzled, even the cleaner pulled a face!

Bob continued with his story; of Amy, the flying ace…

"…Amy was born in 1903,

When women stayed home and made the tea,

Washed the dishes, and raised the kids,

So dads could earn the money."

Amy went to school then University: working hard for her degree,
But she only ever wanted to fly; have adventures, be brave and free.

So she gained her pilot's licence and also in the same year,

Amy became the first British woman to qualify as a ground engineer.

Not only could she fly a plane, she fixed them when they broke.

Fuelled them up and changed their oil, unheard of by womenfolk!

Amy desperately needed a plane but money was ever so tight.

So Daddy chipped in with a businessman;

Amy's dream was now in sight.

They paid for Jason the Gypsy Moth,

Wood and cloth, with two small wings.

It would fly Amy all over the world,

And could do loops, twists and spins!

Josie was feeling much happier now,

The turbo Twins had disappeared,

And Colin the cleaner was sipping his coffee,

He now had a frothy beard.

Bob shared more of Amy's adventures,

How she flew across the land,

With little ore than a map and compass

And no-one to hold her hand…

…No mobile phone or Sat - Nav, no canopy to keep her dry.

Just a coat and a pair of goggles

To stop the wind from making her cry!

Amy did an extraordinary thing, in 1930 on the 5th of May,

When she took off from Croydon Airport, scared but on her way.

Very few people waved her off, but the papers did give her a mention.

Then word got out as Amy flew all about and soon drew a lot of attention.

On her way to sunny Oz,

And her life wouldn't be the same.

After Amy flew 10 hours a day and thousands of miles in her plane.

Through the storms she battled and the shark infested sea,
Crashing her way to Darwin, Australia; Amy became a celebrity.

"...Because no other woman had done it,

And Amy had done it solo,

By flying from London to Australia, and the first woman pilot to do so.

"Amy was given cars and planes, the King gave her special praise,

During a 6-week tour of Australia, with 47 speeches in just 4 days!

Amy also broke flying records and flew during World War 2.

She was happy serving her King and country…

Then into the clouds she flew…"

Said Bob to Josie, as he looked around,

But Josie was up in the sky…

Josie the Jet had found her wings as she happily looped and twirled,

Wondering how good Amy had felt as she flew across the world.

Colin the cleaner clapped and cheered,

As Bob took him for a ride,

High above the fluffy clouds, a spare propeller strapped to the side.

Amy's story taught Josie a lesson;

Believe in yourself and never give up,

Don't worry what people think,

Be first, they'll soon catch up!

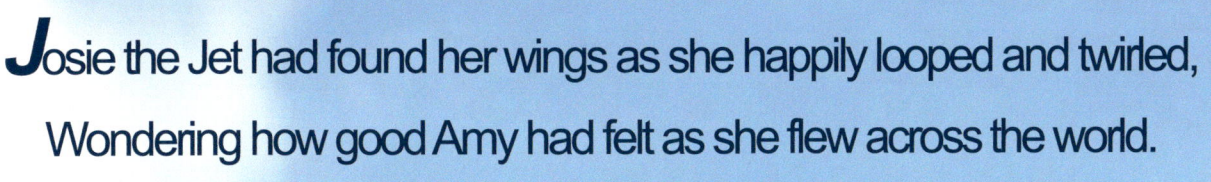

Can you help Amy to find the right answers in this fun quiz?

1) Who or what was Josie?

A) A jester   B) A joker   C) A little jet

2) What was Josie afraid of?

A) Fleas   B) Fairies   C) Flying

3) What was Bob?

A) A beetle   B) A bumble bee   C) A biplane

4) What colour were the Turbo Twins?

A) Blue   B) Burgundy   C) Red

5) What did Amy call her little plane?

A) JamieB) JuliaC) Jason

6) What was Jason made of?

A) MetalB) PlasticC) Wood and cloth

7) What was the sea infested with?

A) SalmonB) ShrimpC) Sharks

8) How many speeches did Amy give in just 4 days?

A) 4B) 400C) 47

The answers are below. Turn the book upside down to read them.

Answers: The correct answers are all C